I0009751

Mastering Natural Language Processing (NLP)

By Farhana Sethi

Natural Language Processing (NLP) is a branch of artificial intelligence that enables machines to understand, interpret, and generate human language. From virtual assistants like Siri and Alexa to advanced chatbots and automated translation systems, NLP plays a crucial role in modern technology. This book aims to provide a comprehensive guide to NLP, covering its fundamentals, advanced techniques, applications, and the future of language technology.

NLP is a transformative technology shaping industries. With ongoing advancements in deep learning, multimodal AI, and ethical considerations, its potential will continue to grow. Understanding NLP equips professionals with the tools to innovate in AI-driven communication.

With continuous research and ethical considerations, NLP will continue to shape the digital world, enabling machines to process language with near-human proficiency.

Contents

Dedication

To my family, whose unwavering support has been the cornerstone of my journey

About me

I am a multifaceted professional—business leader, technical researcher, writer, developer, and digital content curator—with 20 years of experience in the technology sector. As a Computer Engineer and Technology Leader, I am driven by the endless possibilities of technology, astrophysics, and human psychology. My passion for exploration has taken me to six continents and over 40 countries, and I've had the privilege of living and working on three continents. These experiences have enriched my perspective, deepened my understanding of diverse cultures, and fuelled my passion for innovation.

My mission is to bridge technology and humanity, leveraging my expertise to foster meaningful progress, collaboration, and innovation in a world that continues to evolve. Through my work, I strive to inspire others, embrace diverse perspectives, and create solutions that not only advance technology but also improve the lives of people around the globe.

Why I Wrote This Book

Writing a book on Natural Language Processing (NLP) can be a rewarding endeavor for several reasons:

1. **Knowledge Sharing**: By writing this book, you can share your expertise and insights with others who are interested in NLP. It can serve as a valuable resource for students, researchers, and professionals looking to learn more about the field.

2. **Professional Growth**: Authoring a book can enhance your professional reputation and credibility. It demonstrates your deep understanding of NLP and your ability to communicate complex concepts effectively.

3. **Educational Impact**: Your book can be used as a textbook or reference material in academic courses, helping to educate the next generation of NLP practitioners and researchers.

4. **Contribution to the Field**: By documenting the latest techniques, challenges, and trends in NLP, you contribute to the ongoing development and advancement of the field. Your insights and perspectives can inspire new research and innovations.

5. **Personal Fulfillment**: Writing a book can be a personally fulfilling experience. It allows you to reflect on your knowledge, organize your thoughts, and create something lasting that can benefit others.

6. **Addressing Gaps**: If you have identified gaps or areas that are not well-covered in existing literature, your book can fill those gaps and provide comprehensive coverage of important topics.

7. **Community Engagement**: Engaging with the NLP community through your book can lead to new connections, collaborations, and opportunities to participate in discussions and events related to NLP.

Ultimately, writing this book allows you to make a meaningful contribution to the field of NLP while also achieving personal and professional growth.

Who should read this book

This book on Natural Language Processing (NLP) is designed for a wide range of readers, including:

1. **Students**: Undergraduate and graduate students studying computer science, data science, artificial intelligence, or related fields will find this book valuable for understanding the fundamentals and advanced concepts of NLP.

2. **Researchers**: Academics and researchers working in NLP or related areas can use this book as a reference to stay updated on the latest techniques, challenges, and trends in the field.

3. **Professionals**: Data scientists, machine learning engineers, and software developers who are involved in NLP projects will benefit from the practical applications and detailed explanations provided in the book.

4. **Educators**: Professors and instructors can use this book as a textbook or supplementary material for courses on NLP, machine learning, or artificial intelligence.

5. **Enthusiasts**: Individuals with a keen interest in NLP and AI, even if they are not formally studying or working in the field, will find this book accessible and informative.

6. **Business Leaders**: Executives and managers who want to understand how NLP can be applied to improve business processes, customer service, and market analysis will gain valuable insights from this book.

7. **Content Moderators**: Professionals involved in content moderation and social media management can learn about NLP techniques for detecting and managing inappropriate content.

8. **Healthcare Professionals**: Those in the healthcare industry can explore how NLP can be used to analyze medical records, patient feedback, and research literature.

By catering to these diverse audiences, the book aims to provide comprehensive coverage of NLP concepts and applications, making it a valuable resource for anyone interested in the field.

Chapter 1: Introduction to NLP

What is NLP?

Natural Language Processing (NLP) is an interdisciplinary field that combines linguistics, computer science, and artificial intelligence to facilitate communication between humans and computers using natural language. NLP allows machines to read, analyze, and generate text in ways that mimic human understanding.

At its core, NLP bridges the gap between human communication and machine intelligence. It enables computers to process and understand large volumes of textual data, making them capable of performing tasks like translation, summarization, speech recognition, sentiment analysis, and even conversational AI.

With the exponential growth of digital communication, the ability to analyze, interpret, and respond to human language has become more critical than ever. NLP powers applications such as search engines, recommendation systems, customer support automation, and content moderation, revolutionizing industries worldwide.

History and Evolution of NLP

The journey of NLP began in the 1950s with rule-based systems and has evolved significantly with machine learning and deep learning advancements. Some key milestones in NLP history include:

- **1950s-60s**: Early rule-based translation systems emerged, influenced by computational linguistics and Noam Chomsky's theories of syntax. The Georgetown-IBM experiment in 1954 demonstrated the first machine translation system.

- **1970s-80s**: Development of statistical models for speech and text processing led to the introduction of Hidden Markov Models (HMMs), which were used in speech recognition and text categorization.

- **1990s-2000s**: The rise of machine learning techniques, including support vector machines (SVMs) and Naïve Bayes classifiers, allowed for more accurate text classification, named entity recognition, and sentiment analysis.

- **2010s-present**: Deep learning and transformer-based models like BERT, GPT, and T5 revolutionized the field. These models achieved state-of-the-art performance in tasks like machine translation, text summarization, and conversational AI.

Importance of NLP in AI

NLP is at the core of many AI applications, playing a pivotal role in how humans interact with machines. Some of the most significant contributions of NLP include:

- **Chatbots & Virtual Assistants**: AI-powered assistants like Google Assistant, Amazon Alexa, and Apple's Siri use NLP to understand spoken language, process user queries, and respond appropriately. These virtual assistants rely on advanced NLP models to interpret intent and provide meaningful responses.

- **Sentiment Analysis**: Businesses leverage sentiment analysis to gauge customer opinions and brand perception by analyzing social media posts, reviews, and survey responses. This application helps companies make data-driven decisions.

- **Machine Translation**: NLP-powered translation systems, such as Google Translate and DeepL, enable cross-language communication by translating text from one language to another with increasing accuracy.

- **Speech Recognition**: Speech-to-text systems convert spoken language into written text, facilitating applications like voice-controlled assistants, transcription services, and real-time captioning for accessibility.

- **Text Summarization**: NLP techniques allow automated summarization of lengthy documents, news articles, and reports, saving time and effort in extracting key insights.

- **Information Retrieval**: Search engines like Google rely on NLP to index, retrieve, and rank relevant documents based on user queries, improving search accuracy and relevance.

- **Named Entity Recognition (NER)**: Identifies key entities (people, organizations, locations) within text, enabling applications such as automated data extraction and content tagging.

- **Conversational AI & Dialogue Systems**: NLP-driven systems like OpenAI's ChatGPT and Microsoft's DialoGPT create human-like conversational agents capable of engaging in meaningful discussions across various domains.

Key Challenges in NLP

While NLP has made significant progress, several challenges remain in making machines truly understand human language:

- **Ambiguity**: Words and phrases often have multiple meanings depending on context. For example, the word "bank" can refer to a financial institution or the side of a river.

- **Sarcasm & Irony**: Detecting sarcasm and irony remains difficult for machines, as they rely on contextual understanding and tone.

- **Language Evolution**: Human languages continuously evolve, incorporating slang, abbreviations, and new terms, making it challenging to keep NLP models updated.

- **Code-Switching & Multilingualism**: Many users mix multiple languages in conversations (e.g., "Spanglish" or "Hinglish"), requiring NLP models to handle code-switching efficiently.

- **Bias in NLP Models**: AI models trained on biased datasets can produce discriminatory results, necessitating ethical considerations in model development.

- **Computational Complexity**: Training large-scale NLP models requires vast computational resources, raising concerns about accessibility and energy consumption.

Current Trends and Future Directions

NLP is a rapidly evolving field with ongoing advancements that continue to push the boundaries of language understanding. Some of the current trends shaping the future of NLP include:

- **Transformer-Based Models**: The dominance of transformer architectures like BERT, GPT, and T5 has led to state-of-the-art performance in NLP tasks. Researchers continue to refine these models to improve efficiency and interpretability.

- **Multimodal NLP**: Integrating text with other modalities such as images and audio to enable richer interactions, as seen in models like CLIP and DALL·E.

- **Few-Shot and Zero-Shot Learning**: Developing models that require minimal training examples to generalize across multiple tasks, reducing data dependency.

- **Ethical AI & Bias Mitigation**: Addressing biases in NLP models to ensure fairness, transparency, and responsible AI deployment.

- **Real-Time NLP Applications**: Enhancing real-time language processing capabilities in areas like live translation, automated summarization, and AI-driven customer support.

NLP is at the forefront of AI-driven innovation, impacting industries ranging from healthcare and finance to entertainment and education. As the field progresses, researchers and developers continue to refine NLP models, pushing towards more accurate, context-aware, and ethical AI systems.

This book will explore these applications in detail and provide hands-on examples to help you master NLP techniques.

Chapter 2: Fundamentals of NLP

Text Preprocessing

Before applying NLP techniques, raw text data must be preprocessed. Common preprocessing steps include:

- **Tokenization**: Splitting text into words or sentences. Tokenization is an essential step in NLP, breaking text into meaningful components. This step is crucial for further text analysis, machine learning tasks, and deep learning models. Tokenization can be word-based or sentence-based, depending on the requirement.

- **Stopword Removal**: Eliminating common words like "the" and "is" that do not add meaningful value. Removing stopwords helps reduce noise in text processing tasks. However, in some contexts, stopwords may carry significance, requiring careful selection based on the task.

- **Stemming and Lemmatization**: Reducing words to their root forms (e.g., "running" → "run"). Stemming applies heuristic rules to strip suffixes, while lemmatization utilizes vocabulary knowledge and morphological analysis to get base forms.

- **Lowercasing**: Converting text to lowercase to maintain consistency. This step helps standardize the text for processing and comparison, ensuring uniformity.

- **Removing Punctuation and Special Characters**: Cleaning text for better analysis. Punctuation marks and symbols often do not carry significance in NLP tasks and may need removal, except in cases where punctuation holds meaning (e.g., sentiment analysis).
- **Handling Missing Data**: Strategies to deal with incomplete datasets. Missing data can arise due to various reasons, such as human error, transmission issues, or improper data collection. Handling missing data efficiently ensures the quality and reliability of NLP models.

Text Representation Techniques

After preprocessing, text data needs to be transformed into a structured representation that can be processed by machine learning models. Some key techniques include:

- **Bag of Words (BoW)**: A simple representation where text is converted into a set of words, ignoring grammar and word order but retaining frequency.
- **TF-IDF (Term Frequency-Inverse Document Frequency)**: Measures the importance of a word in a document relative to a collection of documents.
- **Word Embeddings (Word2Vec, GloVe, FastText)**: Capturing semantic relationships between words by mapping them to high-dimensional vectors.
- **Sentence Embeddings (BERT, GPT, T5)**: Advanced deep learning models that create contextualized embeddings for sentences and paragraphs.

Feature Engineering in NLP

Feature engineering plays a crucial role in building effective NLP models. Some common features include:

- **N-grams**: Capturing sequences of words (e.g., bigrams, trigrams) to retain context.
- **Part-of-Speech (POS) Tagging**: Assigning grammatical tags (e.g., noun, verb, adjective) to words.
- **Named Entity Recognition (NER)**: Identifying entities such as names, dates, locations.
- **Syntax and Dependency Parsing**: Analyzing sentence structure and grammatical relationships.

Text Normalization and Noise Reduction

Text normalization involves transforming text into a standard format, ensuring consistency and reducing unnecessary variations. Common techniques include:

- **Expanding Contractions**: Converting "don't" to "do not" and "can't" to "cannot."
- **Correcting Spelling Errors**: Using algorithms to identify and fix misspelled words.
- **Removing HTML Tags and URLs**: Eliminating unnecessary elements from web-scraped text data.

Tokenization and Sentence Segmentation in Depth

Tokenization involves breaking text into smaller meaningful units. It plays a fundamental role in many NLP applications:

- **Word Tokenization**: Splitting text into individual words.
- **Sentence Tokenization**: Dividing text into meaningful sentence-level segments.
- **Subword Tokenization (Byte Pair Encoding - BPE, WordPiece)**: Breaking words into smaller subword units, crucial for handling rare words and improving language model performance.

Common NLP Libraries and Tools

Several powerful libraries facilitate NLP tasks:

- **NLTK (Natural Language Toolkit)**: Provides extensive tools for NLP processing.

- **spaCy**: Efficient NLP library optimized for deep learning.

- **Gensim**: Specializes in topic modeling and document similarity.

- **Transformers (Hugging Face)**: Offers pre-trained deep learning models for various NLP applications.

By understanding these fundamental concepts, we lay the groundwork for more advanced NLP topics, including machine learning-based NLP, deep learning models, and real-world applications.

Chapter 3: Machine Learning in NLP

Supervised vs. Unsupervised Learning

Machine learning in NLP can be broadly categorized into supervised and unsupervised learning:

- **Supervised Learning**: Involves training a model on labeled data, where each input has a corresponding output. Common tasks include text classification, sentiment analysis, and named entity recognition.

- **Unsupervised Learning**: Involves training a model on unlabeled data, where the algorithm tries to find patterns and relationships. Common tasks include clustering, topic modeling, and anomaly detection.

Classification Algorithms

Classification algorithms are used to categorize text into predefined classes. Here are some commonly used algorithms:

- **Naive Bayes**: A probabilistic classifier based on Bayes' theorem, assuming independence between features. It's simple and effective for text classification.

- **Support Vector Machines (SVM)**: A powerful classifier that finds the optimal hyperplane to separate classes. It's effective for high-dimensional data.

- **Decision Trees**: A tree-like model that splits data based on feature values. It's easy to interpret and can handle both categorical and numerical data.

Clustering Algorithms

Clustering algorithms group similar texts together. Here are some commonly used algorithms:

- **K-means**: Partitions data into k clusters based on similarity. It's simple and efficient but requires specifying the number of clusters.

- **Hierarchical Clustering**: Builds a hierarchy of clusters using either agglomerative (bottom-up) or divisive (top-down) approaches. It doesn't require specifying the number of clusters.

Text Classification Techniques in Detail

1. **Naive Bayes**:
   - **Multinomial Naive Bayes**: Suitable for text data, where features are word frequencies.
   - **Bernoulli Naive Bayes**: Suitable for binary features, where presence or absence of words is considered.

2. **Support Vector Machines (SVM)**:
   - **Linear SVM**: Effective for linearly separable data.
   - **Kernel SVM**: Uses kernel functions (e.g., RBF, polynomial) to handle non-linear data.

3. **Decision Trees**:
   - **CART (Classification and Regression Trees)**: Splits data based on feature values to create a tree structure.
   - **Random Forests**: An ensemble method that builds multiple decision trees and averages their predictions.

Clustering Techniques in Detail

1. **K-means**:
   - **Initialization**: Choosing initial cluster centers (e.g., k-means++, random).
   - **Iteration**: Assigning points to clusters and updating cluster centers until convergence.

2. **Hierarchical Clustering**:
   - **Agglomerative**: Starts with individual points and merges them into clusters.
   - **Divisive**: Starts with all points in one cluster and splits them into smaller clusters.

Practical Applications

- **Text Classification**: Using supervised learning algorithms to categorize emails as spam or not spam.
- **Sentiment Analysis**: Classifying text as positive, negative, or neutral using machine learning models.
- **Topic Modeling**: Using unsupervised learning algorithms to identify topics in a collection of documents.

Example: Sentiment Analysis with Naive Bayes

1. **Data Preparation**: Collect and preprocess text data (e.g., tweets, reviews).
2. **Feature Extraction**: Convert text into numerical features using techniques like TF-IDF.
3. **Model Training**: Train a Naive Bayes classifier on labeled data.
4. **Prediction**: Use the trained model to predict sentiment of new text data.

Chapter 4: Deep Learning in NLP

Introduction to Neural Networks

Neural networks are a key component of deep learning. They consist of layers of interconnected nodes (neurons) that process input data to produce output. Here are some basic concepts:

- **Layers**: Input layer, hidden layers, and output layer.

- **Activation Functions**: Functions like ReLU, sigmoid, and tanh that introduce non-linearity into the model.

- **Training**: The process of adjusting weights using algorithms like backpropagation and optimization techniques like gradient descent.

Recurrent Neural Networks (RNNs)

RNNs are designed to handle sequential data, making them ideal for NLP tasks. They maintain a hidden state that captures information from previous time steps. Key concepts include:

- **Vanishing Gradient Problem**: Difficulty in training RNNs due to gradients becoming very small.

- **Long Short-Term Memory (LSTM)**: A type of RNN that addresses the vanishing gradient problem by using gates to control the flow of information.

- **Gated Recurrent Unit (GRU)**: Similar to LSTM but with fewer gates, making it computationally efficient.

Transformers and BERT

Transformers have revolutionized NLP by enabling parallel processing of data, leading to faster and more accurate models. Key concepts include:

- **Attention Mechanism**: Allows the model to focus on relevant parts of the input sequence.

- **Encoder-Decoder Architecture**: Used in tasks like machine translation, where the encoder processes the input and the decoder generates the output.

- **BERT (Bidirectional Encoder Representations from Transformers)**: A pre-trained model that captures context from both directions, leading to improved performance on various NLP tasks.

Deep Learning Techniques in Detail

1. **Neural Networks**:

   - **Feedforward Neural Networks**: Basic type of neural network where information flows in one direction.

   - **Convolutional Neural Networks (CNNs)**: Typically used for image processing but can be applied to text data for tasks like sentence classification.

2. **Recurrent Neural Networks (RNNs)**:

   - **Standard RNNs**: Maintain a hidden state that captures information from previous time steps.

   - **LSTM Networks**: Use gates to control the flow of information, addressing the vanishing gradient problem.

   - **GRU Networks**: Similar to LSTM but with fewer gates, making them computationally efficient.

3. **Transformers**:

   - **Self-Attention Mechanism**: Allows the model to focus on relevant parts of the input sequence.

   - **Encoder-Decoder Architecture**: Used in tasks like machine translation, where the encoder processes the input and the decoder generates the output.

   - **BERT**: A pre-trained model that captures context from both directions, leading to improved performance on various NLP tasks.

Practical Applications

- **Text Generation**: Using RNNs and LSTMs to generate coherent text based on input sequences.

- **Machine Translation**: Using transformers and encoder-decoder architectures to translate text from one language to another.

- **Question Answering Systems**: Using BERT to understand and answer questions based on context.

Example: Text Generation with LSTM

1. **Data Preparation**: Collect and preprocess text data (e.g., books, articles).

2. **Model Architecture**: Build an LSTM network with input, hidden, and output layers.

3. **Training**: Train the model on the text data, adjusting weights using backpropagation.

4. **Generation**: Use the trained model to generate new text based on input sequences.

Chapter 5: Advanced NLP Applications

Sentiment Analysis

Sentiment analysis involves determining the sentiment expressed in a piece of text, such as positive, negative, or neutral. It's widely used in social media monitoring, customer feedback analysis, and market research.

- **Techniques**:
  - **Lexicon-based methods**: Use predefined lists of words associated with positive or negative sentiments.
  - **Machine learning methods**: Train classifiers like Naive Bayes, SVM, or deep learning models on labeled sentiment data.
  - **Hybrid methods**: Combine lexicon-based and machine learning approaches for improved accuracy.

Machine Translation

Machine translation involves automatically translating text from one language to another. It's used in applications like Google Translate and multilingual customer support.

- **Techniques**:
  - **Rule-based translation**: Uses linguistic rules and dictionaries to translate text.
  - **Statistical machine translation (SMT)**: Uses statistical models based on bilingual text corpora.
  - **Neural machine translation (NMT)**: Uses deep learning models, particularly transformers, to translate text with high accuracy.

Text Summarization

Text summarization involves creating a concise summary of a longer text. It's used in news aggregation, document summarization, and content curation.

- **Techniques**:
  - **Extractive summarization**: Selects key sentences or phrases from the original text.
  - **Abstractive summarization**: Generates new sentences that capture the essence of the original text using deep learning models.

Question Answering Systems

Question answering systems involve answering questions posed in natural language. They are used in search engines, virtual assistants, and customer support bots.

- **Techniques**:
  - **Information retrieval-based**: Retrieves relevant documents and extracts answers.
  - **Knowledge-based**: Uses structured knowledge bases to find answers.
  - **Machine learning-based**: Uses models like BERT to understand context and generate answers.

Advanced NLP Techniques in Detail

1. **Sentiment Analysis**:
   - **Lexicon-based methods**: Use sentiment dictionaries like SentiWordNet.
   - **Machine learning methods**: Train classifiers on labeled sentiment data using features like TF-IDF or word embeddings.
   - **Hybrid methods**: Combine lexicon-based and machine learning approaches for improved accuracy.

2. **Machine Translation**:
   - **Rule-based translation**: Uses linguistic rules and dictionaries to translate text.
   - **Statistical machine translation (SMT)**: Uses statistical models based on bilingual text corpora.
   - **Neural machine translation (NMT)**: Uses deep learning models, particularly transformers, to translate text with high accuracy.

3. **Text Summarization**:
   - **Extractive summarization**: Selects key sentences or phrases from the original text.
   - **Abstractive summarization**: Generates new sentences that capture the essence of the original text using deep learning models.

4. **Question Answering Systems**:
   - **Information retrieval-based**: Retrieves relevant documents and extracts answers.
   - **Knowledge-based**: Uses structured knowledge bases to find answers.
   - **Machine learning-based**: Uses models like BERT to understand context and generate answers.

Practical Applications

- **Sentiment Analysis**: Monitoring social media for brand sentiment, analyzing customer reviews for product feedback.
- **Machine Translation**: Translating websites and documents for multilingual audiences, providing real-time translation in chat applications.
- **Text Summarization**: Summarizing news articles for quick reading, creating executive summaries of reports.
- **Question Answering Systems**: Enhancing search engines with direct answers, building virtual assistants that can answer user queries.

Example: Machine Translation with Transformers

1. **Data Preparation**: Collect and preprocess bilingual text corpora.

2. **Model Architecture**: Build a transformer model with encoder and decoder layers.

3. **Training**: Train the model on the bilingual text data, adjusting weights using backpropagation.

4. **Translation**: Use the trained model to translate new text from one language to another.

Chapter 6: Challenges in NLP

Ambiguity and Context

Ambiguity in language is a significant challenge in NLP. Words and sentences can have multiple meanings depending on the context. Here are some types of ambiguity:

- **Lexical Ambiguity**: When a word has multiple meanings. For example, "bank" can refer to a financial institution or the side of a river.

- **Syntactic Ambiguity**: When a sentence can be parsed in multiple ways. For example, "I saw the man with the telescope" can mean either the speaker used a telescope to see the man or the man had a telescope.

- **Semantic Ambiguity**: When the meaning of a sentence is unclear. For example, "Visiting relatives can be annoying" can mean either the act of visiting relatives is annoying or the relatives who visit are annoying.

Sarcasm and Irony

Sarcasm and irony are challenging for NLP models because they involve saying the opposite of what is meant. Detecting sarcasm requires understanding context, tone, and sometimes cultural references.

- **Example**: "Great, another rainy day!" might be sarcastic if the speaker dislikes rain.

Multilingual Processing

Handling multiple languages is a complex task in NLP. Each language has its own syntax, grammar, and idiomatic expressions. Challenges include:

- **Translation**: Ensuring accurate translation while preserving meaning and context.

- **Cross-lingual Information Retrieval**: Retrieving relevant information across different languages.

- **Multilingual Sentiment Analysis**: Analyzing sentiment in texts written in different languages.

Ethical Considerations

Ethical considerations are crucial in NLP, especially as models become more powerful and widespread. Key issues include:

- **Bias and Fairness**: NLP models can inherit biases from training data, leading to unfair or discriminatory outcomes. It's essential to identify and mitigate biases in data and models.

- **Privacy**: Ensuring the privacy of individuals' data used in NLP applications. This includes anonymizing data and adhering to data protection regulations.

- **Misuse**: Preventing the misuse of NLP technologies, such as generating fake news or deepfake content.

Challenges in Detail

1. **Ambiguity and Context**:

   - **Lexical Ambiguity**: Techniques like word sense disambiguation (WSD) can help determine the correct meaning of a word based on context.

   - **Syntactic Ambiguity**: Parsing algorithms and context-aware models can help resolve syntactic ambiguity.

- **Semantic Ambiguity**: Semantic analysis and context-aware models can help clarify the meaning of ambiguous sentences.

2. **Sarcasm and Irony**:

   - **Detection Techniques**: Machine learning models can be trained on labeled data to detect sarcasm. Features like punctuation, word choice, and context can be used.

   - **Challenges**: Sarcasm detection remains difficult due to the subtlety and variability of sarcastic expressions.

3. **Multilingual Processing**:

   - **Translation Models**: Neural machine translation models like transformers can handle multiple languages.

   - **Cross-lingual Techniques**: Techniques like cross-lingual embeddings can help in retrieving information across languages.

   - **Multilingual Sentiment Analysis**: Models can be trained on multilingual data to analyze sentiment in different languages.

4. **Ethical Considerations**:

   - **Bias and Fairness**: Techniques like adversarial training and fairness-aware algorithms can help mitigate biases.

   - **Privacy**: Data anonymization and adherence to regulations like GDPR can help protect privacy.

   - **Misuse Prevention**: Developing guidelines and monitoring the use of NLP technologies can help prevent misuse.

Practical Applications

- **Ambiguity Resolution**: Improving search engines and virtual assistants by resolving ambiguities in user queries.

- **Sarcasm Detection**: Enhancing sentiment analysis tools to better understand user feedback.

- **Multilingual Processing**: Building applications that support multiple languages for global users.

- **Ethical NLP**: Developing fair and unbiased models for applications like hiring and loan approval.

Example: Bias Mitigation in NLP Models

1. **Data Analysis**: Analyze training data for potential biases.

2. **Model Training**: Use techniques like adversarial training to reduce biases in the model.

3. **Evaluation**: Evaluate the model on diverse datasets to ensure fairness.

4. **Deployment**: Monitor the model's performance and make adjustments as needed to maintain fairness.

Chapter: 7 Sentiment Analysis in NLP

Introduction to Sentiment Analysis

Sentiment analysis, also known as opinion mining, is the process of determining the sentiment expressed in a piece of text. It involves classifying text as positive, negative, or neutral. Sentiment analysis is widely used in various applications, including social media monitoring, customer feedback analysis, and market research.

Techniques for Sentiment Analysis

There are several techniques used for sentiment analysis, ranging from simple lexicon-based methods to advanced machine learning and deep learning approaches.

1. **Lexicon-based Methods**

   - **Sentiment Lexicons**: These are predefined lists of words associated with positive or negative sentiments. Examples include SentiWordNet and VADER (Valence Aware Dictionary and sEntiment Reasoner).

   - **Rule-based Approaches**: These methods use linguistic rules to determine sentiment based on the presence of sentiment words and their context.

2. **Machine Learning Methods**

   - **Supervised Learning**: Involves training a classifier on labeled data. Common algorithms include Naive Bayes, Support Vector Machines (SVM), and logistic regression.

   - **Feature Extraction**: Text is converted into numerical features using techniques like Bag of Words (BoW), TF-IDF, or word embeddings (Word2Vec, GloVe).

3. **Deep Learning Methods**

   - **Recurrent Neural Networks (RNNs)**: These models are designed to handle sequential data and can capture context over time. Long Short-Term Memory (LSTM) networks are a popular choice for sentiment analysis.

   - **Convolutional Neural Networks (CNNs)**: Although typically used for image processing, CNNs can also be applied to text data for sentiment classification.

   - **Transformers**: Models like BERT (Bidirectional Encoder Representations from Transformers) have achieved state-of-the-art performance in sentiment analysis by capturing context from both directions.

Steps in Sentiment Analysis

1. **Data Collection**

   - Collect text data from various sources such as social media, reviews, and surveys.

   - Ensure the data is representative of the domain and sentiment classes.

2. **Data Preprocessing**

   - **Tokenization**: Splitting text into individual words or tokens.

   - **Lowercasing**: Converting all text to lowercase to ensure uniformity.

   - **Stop Words Removal**: Removing common words that do not contribute much meaning.

   - **Stemming and Lemmatization**: Reducing words to their root or base form.

3. **Feature Extraction**

   - Convert text into numerical features using techniques like BoW, TF-IDF, or word embeddings.

4. **Model Training**

   - Train a machine learning or deep learning model on the preprocessed and feature-extracted data.

   - Use labeled data to supervise the training process.

5. **Model Evaluation**

   - Evaluate the model's performance using metrics like accuracy, precision, recall, and F1-score.

   - Use a separate test set to ensure the model generalizes well to unseen data.

6. **Prediction**

   - Use the trained model to predict sentiment on new, unseen text data.

Challenges in Sentiment Analysis

- **Sarcasm and Irony**: Detecting sarcasm and irony is challenging because they involve saying the opposite of what is meant.

- **Context and Ambiguity**: Words can have different sentiments depending on the context. For example, "unpredictable" can be positive in the context of a thriller movie but negative in the context of a car's performance.

- **Domain-Specific Sentiment**: Sentiment words can have different meanings in different domains. For example, "sick" can be negative in general but positive in the context of extreme sports.

Applications of Sentiment Analysis

- **Social Media Monitoring**: Analyzing public sentiment on social media platforms to gauge public opinion on various topics.

- **Customer Feedback Analysis**: Understanding customer sentiment from reviews and feedback to improve products and services.

- **Market Research**: Analyzing sentiment in market data to identify trends and make informed business decisions.

Example: Sentiment Analysis with BERT

1. **Data Collection**: Collect a dataset of text reviews labeled with sentiment (positive, negative, neutral).

2. **Data Preprocessing**: Tokenize the text, convert to lowercase, and remove stop words.

3. **Feature Extraction**: Use BERT to convert text into contextual embeddings.

4. **Model Training**: Fine-tune a pre-trained BERT model on the labeled dataset.

5. **Model Evaluation**: Evaluate the model's performance on a test set using metrics like accuracy and F1-score.

6. **Prediction**: Use the fine-tuned BERT model to predict sentiment on new text data.

Chapter: 8 NLP in Social Media

Introduction to NLP in Social Media

Social media platforms like Twitter, Facebook, Instagram, and LinkedIn generate vast amounts of text data daily. Natural Language Processing (NLP) plays a crucial role in analyzing this data to extract valuable insights. Applications of NLP in social media include sentiment analysis, trend detection, user profiling, and content moderation.

Applications of NLP in Social Media

1. **Sentiment Analysis**

    - **Purpose**: Understanding public sentiment towards brands, products, events, and topics.

    - **Techniques**: Lexicon-based methods, machine learning classifiers, and deep learning models like BERT.

    - **Challenges**: Handling sarcasm, slang, and context-specific language.

2. **Trend Detection**

    - **Purpose**: Identifying emerging trends and topics of interest on social media.

- **Techniques**: Topic modeling (e.g., Latent Dirichlet Allocation), clustering algorithms, and keyword extraction.
- **Challenges**: Dealing with noisy data and rapidly changing trends.

3. **User Profiling**

- **Purpose**: Creating detailed profiles of users based on their social media activity.
- **Techniques**: Text classification, entity recognition, and sentiment analysis.
- **Challenges**: Ensuring privacy and ethical considerations.

4. **Content Moderation**

- **Purpose**: Detecting and removing inappropriate or harmful content.
- **Techniques**: Text classification, keyword filtering, and machine learning models.
- **Challenges**: Balancing moderation with freedom of expression and handling diverse languages and contexts.

Techniques for NLP in Social Media

1. **Text Preprocessing**

- **Tokenization**: Splitting text into individual words or tokens.
- **Lowercasing**: Converting all text to lowercase for uniformity.
- **Stop Words Removal**: Removing common words that do not contribute much meaning.
- **Stemming and Lemmatization**: Reducing words to their root or base form.
- **Handling Emojis and Hashtags**: Converting emojis and hashtags into meaningful text representations.

2. **Feature Extraction**

- **Bag of Words (BoW)**: Representing text as a collection of words.
- **TF-IDF (Term Frequency-Inverse Document Frequency)**: Measuring the importance of words in a document relative to a collection of documents.
- **Word Embeddings**: Dense vector representations of words that capture their meanings (e.g., Word2Vec, GloVe).

3. **Machine Learning Models**

- **Supervised Learning**: Training classifiers on labeled data for tasks like sentiment analysis and content moderation.
- **Unsupervised Learning**: Using clustering and topic modeling to detect trends and group similar content.

4. **Deep Learning Models**

- **Recurrent Neural Networks (RNNs)**: Handling sequential data and capturing context over time.
- **Convolutional Neural Networks (CNNs)**: Applying to text data for tasks like sentiment classification.

- **Transformers**: Using models like BERT for state-of-the-art performance in various NLP tasks.

Challenges in NLP for Social Media

1. **Data Quality**

   - **Noisy Data**: Social media text often contains typos, slang, and informal language.
   - **Short Texts**: Tweets and posts are often short, making it challenging to extract meaningful information.

2. **Real-time Processing**

   - **Scalability**: Handling large volumes of data in real-time requires efficient algorithms and infrastructure.
   - **Latency**: Ensuring low latency for real-time applications like trend detection and content moderation.

3. **Multilingual Data**

   - **Language Diversity**: Social media users post in various languages, requiring models to handle multilingual data.
   - **Code-switching**: Users often switch between languages within a single post, adding complexity to text processing.

4. **Ethical Considerations**

   - **Privacy**: Ensuring user data is handled responsibly and in compliance with regulations.
   - **Bias and Fairness**: Addressing biases in models and ensuring fair treatment of all users.

Practical Applications

- **Brand Monitoring**: Analyzing sentiment and trends related to a brand to inform marketing strategies.
- **Customer Support**: Using sentiment analysis to prioritize and respond to customer queries on social media.
- **Crisis Management**: Detecting negative sentiment and emerging issues in real-time to manage crises effectively.
- **Influencer Analysis**: Identifying key influencers and analyzing their impact on social media.

Example: Sentiment Analysis on Twitter Data

1. **Data Collection**: Collect tweets using Twitter's API, focusing on specific keywords or hashtags.
2. **Data Preprocessing**: Tokenize the text, convert to lowercase, remove stop words, and handle emojis and hashtags.
3. **Feature Extraction**: Use TF-IDF or word embeddings to convert text into numerical features.
4. **Model Training**: Train a sentiment classifier (e.g., logistic regression, SVM, or BERT) on labeled tweet data.
5. **Model Evaluation**: Evaluate the model's performance using metrics like accuracy, precision, recall, and F1-score.
6. **Prediction**: Use the trained model to predict sentiment on new tweets and analyze the results.

Chapter 9: Future of NLP

Emerging Trends

The field of NLP is rapidly evolving, with several emerging trends that are shaping its future:

- **Pre-trained Language Models**: Models like GPT-3, BERT, and their successors have revolutionized NLP by providing powerful pre-trained models that can be fine-tuned for various tasks. These models continue to improve in terms of size, accuracy, and efficiency.

- **Multimodal NLP**: Combining text with other data types like images, audio, and video to create more comprehensive models. This trend is leading to advancements in applications like visual question answering and image captioning.

- **Few-shot and Zero-shot Learning**: Techniques that enable models to perform tasks with very few or no examples. This is particularly useful for tasks with limited labeled data and for adapting models to new domains quickly.

Potential Breakthroughs

Several potential breakthroughs could significantly impact the future of NLP:

- **Universal Language Models**: Developing models that can understand and generate text in multiple languages with high accuracy. This could lead to seamless multilingual communication and translation.

- **Explainable AI**: Creating NLP models that can explain their decisions and predictions in a human-understandable way. This is crucial for building trust and transparency in AI systems.

- **Human-like Conversational Agents**: Advancements in dialogue systems and conversational AI could lead to more natural and human-like interactions with virtual assistants and chatbots.

Impact on Society

The advancements in NLP have the potential to bring about significant societal changes:

- **Education**: NLP can enhance educational tools, providing personalized learning experiences and automated grading systems.

- **Healthcare**: NLP can assist in medical research, patient care, and administrative tasks by analyzing medical records, literature, and patient feedback.

- **Business**: NLP can improve customer service, market analysis, and decision-making processes by analyzing large volumes of text data.

Future Directions in Detail

1. **Pre-trained Language Models**:

    - **GPT-3 and Beyond**: Continued development of larger and more powerful models that can perform a wide range of NLP tasks with minimal fine-tuning.

    - **BERT and Variants**: Improvements in transformer-based models that capture context more effectively and efficiently.

2. **Multimodal NLP**:

    - **Visual Question Answering**: Combining text and image data to answer questions about images.

    - **Image Captioning**: Generating descriptive captions for images using text and visual data.

3. **Few-shot and Zero-shot Learning**:

    - **Few-shot Learning**: Training models to perform tasks with very few labeled examples.

    - **Zero-shot Learning**: Enabling models to perform tasks without any labeled examples by leveraging knowledge from related tasks.

4. **Universal Language Models**:

    - **Multilingual Models**: Developing models that can understand and generate text in multiple languages with high accuracy.

    - **Cross-lingual Transfer Learning**: Transferring knowledge from one language to another to improve performance on low-resource languages.

5. **Explainable AI**:

    - **Model Interpretability**: Creating models that can explain their decisions and predictions in a human-understandable way.

    - **Transparency**: Building trust in AI systems by making their inner workings more transparent.

6. **Human-like Conversational Agents**:

    - **Dialogue Systems**: Advancements in dialogue systems that can handle complex and multi-turn conversations.

    - **Conversational AI**: Creating virtual assistants and chatbots that can interact with users in a natural and human-like manner.

Practical Applications

- **Education**: Personalized learning experiences, automated grading, and intelligent tutoring systems.

- **Healthcare**: Analyzing medical records, literature, and patient feedback to assist in medical research and patient care.

- **Business**: Improving customer service, market analysis, and decision-making processes by analyzing large volumes of text data.

Example: Multimodal NLP for Visual Question Answering

1. **Data Collection**: Collect and preprocess datasets that contain images and corresponding questions.

2. **Model Architecture**: Build a multimodal model that combines text and image data using techniques like transformers and convolutional neural networks (CNNs).

3. **Training**: Train the model on the multimodal dataset, adjusting weights using backpropagation.

4. **Evaluation**: Evaluate the model's performance on a test set and fine-tune as needed.

Conclusion

Natural Language Processing (NLP) is a dynamic and rapidly evolving field that plays a crucial role in enabling computers to understand, interpret, and generate human language. From basic text preprocessing techniques to advanced deep learning models, NLP encompasses a wide range of methods and applications.

In social media, NLP has proven to be invaluable for sentiment analysis, trend detection, user profiling, and content moderation. These applications help businesses and organizations gain insights into public opinion, manage crises, and improve customer support.

Despite its advancements, NLP faces several challenges, including ambiguity, context, sarcasm, multilingual processing, and ethical considerations. Addressing these challenges requires continuous research and development to create more accurate, fair, and transparent models.

Looking ahead, the future of NLP holds exciting possibilities with emerging trends like pre-trained language models, multimodal NLP, few-shot learning, and explainable AI. These advancements will further enhance the capabilities of NLP and its impact on various domains, including education, healthcare, and business.

As NLP continues to evolve, it will undoubtedly play a pivotal role in shaping the way we interact with technology and each other, making our digital experiences more intuitive, personalized, and meaningful.

What's Coming Next

Cybersecurity and Privacy in Generative AI

Generative AI, including models like GPT-3 and DALL-E, introduces significant cybersecurity and privacy challenges alongside its transformative capabilities. On the cybersecurity front, generative AI can be exploited to create sophisticated phishing scams, deepfakes, and self-evolving malware, making traditional defenses less effective. Securing AI systems against threats like model inversion, data poisoning, and adversarial examples is crucial. Privacy concerns arise from risks of re-identification, data leakage during model training, and the potential for behavioral tracking. Mitigation strategies include robust security measures like encryption and access controls, privacy-preserving techniques such as differential privacy and federated learning, and ethical AI development practices to ensure fairness, transparency, and regulatory compliance. Balancing these aspects is essential to harness the benefits of generative AI while safeguarding against its risks.

Purpose

Writing a book about cybersecurity and privacy in generative AI is incredibly important for several reasons. First, it allows me to share essential insights and knowledge on a rapidly evolving topic that affects various industries and individuals. By documenting the challenges and mitigation strategies, I contribute to the broader understanding and responsible use of generative AI. This can help others navigate the complexities of cybersecurity and privacy in AI, making my book a valuable educational resource for students, researchers, and professionals.

Additionally, authoring such a book can enhance my professional reputation, positioning me as an expert in the field. This can open up opportunities for speaking engagements, collaborations, and consulting. Moreover, addressing these critical issues can drive ethical AI development, ensuring that the technology benefits society while safeguarding against potential risks. By writing this book, I can make a meaningful contribution to the field and help shape the future of AI in a positive way.

How to connect with me

I value the opportunity to connect with readers, thinkers, and innovators like you! Whether you have questions, feedback, or are simply looking to continue the conversation, here are some ways to get in touch:

- **Email**: Reach out to me at **Contact@FSethi.com** for inquiries, thoughts, or to share your ideas.
- **Social Media**: Follow and engage with me on Linkedin@fsethi or My YouTube channel @fsethi to stay updated with my latest projects and insights.
- **Website**: Visit https://www.fsethi.com for more resources, upcoming events, and exclusive content related to the book.
- **Newsletter**: Follow me on LinkedIn to my blogs for updates on my work, industry trends, and behind-the-scenes stories. You can follow me at https://www.linkedin.com/in/fsethi/recent-activity/articles/
- **Speaking Engagements**: Interested in hosting a discussion or keynote about generative AI and the energy business? Send an inquiry to **Contact@FSethi.com**

I'm always excited to hear from readers—your thoughts, ideas, and perspectives inspire my work. Let's keep the dialogue going!